SUNDAY MASS

Sunday Mass

OUR ROLE AND WHY IT MATTERS

Anne Y. Koester

LITURGICAL PRESS
Collegeville, Minnesota

www.litpress.org

Nihil Obstat: Robert C. Harren, J.C.L., *Censor deputatus.*

Imprimatur: ✠ John F. Kinney, J.C.D., D.D., Bishop of St. Cloud, October 17, 2006.

Cover design by David Manahan, O.S.B. Photo courtesy of iStockphoto.com, © Ralph Hoppe.

1   2   3   4   5   6   7   8   9

Library of Congress Cataloging-in-Publication Data

Koester, Anne Y.
    Sunday mass : our role and why it matters / Anne Y. Koester.
        p.   cm.
    ISBN-13: 978-0-8146-3163-8
    ISBN-10: 0-8146-3163-0
    1. Religious gatherings—Catholic Church.   2. Sunday.   3. Mass.   4. Public worship—Catholic Church.   I. Title.
    BX1970.15.K64   2007
    264'.02036—dc22
                                                    2006031498

To my parents,

Mary Jane and Alphonse (†1977) Koester,

*my first models and mentors
in the Christian faith*

Contents

Preface

In recent years it has been my privilege to talk with people from a variety of parishes in the United States about their experiences of Sunday Mass. When given the opportunity to speak about the liturgy of the Catholic Church, I always spend time exploring the role of the assembly—specifically, the assembly's ministry and mission.

Time after time people's response to the conversation about their role as the Sunday assembly is wonderfully enthusiastic. Many people tell me that they had never seriously considered the active part they as the assembly play not only during Mass but also after they are sent "in peace to love and serve the Lord" (dismissal). Their newfound awareness opens up the Sunday experience for them, leading them to new insights and enabling them to see new possibilities. They begin paying attention to the assembly itself—all the people of various ages and backgrounds who come together on Sundays because of what they have in common. They begin to understand themselves and all who make up the assembly as the Body of Christ and, consequently, as a people called to be the Body of Christ in the world.

These conversations inspired me to put together this resource, which I hope offers readers an opportunity to reflect on the ministry and mission of the Sunday assembly and to discover all the amazing possibilities that will be revealed in the process.

I must express my gratitude to a good friend, Rev. John Konicek, for his support, creative insights, and careful reading of draft chapters.

Introduction

Why consider *who* goes to Sunday Mass?

There are many reasons to consider *who* goes to Sunday Mass. Three are especially key:

- First, because the *who* is *you* and everyone else who gathers on Sunday to praise and thank God. Each of us and all of us together are needed. There would be no Sunday celebration without us—the assembly, the gathered church.

- Second, because the more we become aware of our role as the assembly, the more rich in meaning the Sunday liturgy can be for us. We might feel more drawn into the celebration, and often when we are drawn into something, the chances are increased that the experience will touch our lives in unexpected and meaningful ways. We might, for example, hear a passage in the gospel reading that gives us new insights into something we are struggling with, or our "Amen" to the Body and Blood of Christ might urge us to reach out to someone in need.

  An involved Sunday assembly can also enhance the celebration itself. For example, we have probably all experienced a Sunday Mass where the people were "just there," that is, putting in their time but not much more. The celebration was likely flat and uninspiring. Now if we compare that Sunday experience with one we have had where the people were *really* there—fully and actively engaged in the Mass, truly present to the presence of Christ and to one another—our response to the experience was likely very different. Perhaps we could sense that the people wanted to be there and knew they had an essential part to play. They were hospitable and welcoming. They sang and responded in good voice; their "Amens" were truly "Amens" and not mindless mumbles. They actively listened; their gestures and movements were thoughtful, not sloppy or robotic. Periods of silence weren't times of impatience or fidgeting but rather a meaningful part of the experience.

I think that by contrasting these two experiences, we instinctively know that getting better acquainted with our role as the Sunday assembly is very important.

- Third, because the more we realize what it means to be the Sunday assembly, the more we will realize that our ministry and mission extend beyond the liturgical celebration itself. Have you ever thought of the Sunday Eucharist as *a time when we practice* how to be and act as baptized people in the world, from our homes to our workplaces to our local and global communities? In other words, we might ask, "What does our role as the Sunday assembly have to do with our role as Christians living in a twenty-first-century world?"

Who's it for?

Everyone! All baptized people belong to the Sunday assembly, so everyone—adult and youth, lay and ordained, regardless of where you feel you are on the journey of faith—is invited to explore this topic. In this book you will find brief commentaries, questions for journaling and conversation, and invitations to tell stories. It is adaptable for use by individuals or groups. Groups might want to designate one or two persons to facilitate the conversations. Working first in smaller groups (of three to five people) is often helpful, followed by conversation with the larger group.

Defining a few words

I want to note a few words that I use interchangeably. When I speak of the church's Sunday worship (which includes the Saturday afternoon/evening anticipated Mass of Sunday), I use the following words or phrases, all of which refer to the same event: *Sunday liturgy* or *celebration* or *worship; Eucharist; eucharistic liturgy or celebration; Mass.* Using these various names is consistent with Catholic tradition. We know from the church's history, for example, that the Sunday gathering has been called Breaking of the

Bread, Communion, Eucharist, the Lord's Supper, Mass (a term that came from the dismissal in the Roman rite during the Middle Ages), oblation (or offering), and of course, liturgy.

The word "liturgy" comes from a Greek word *(leitourgia)* and was used by the Greek-speaking Christians in the early centuries of the church to refer to any act of worship. Unfortunately, the term fell out of use for hundreds of years, was revived in the eighteenth century, and has been used regularly since the Second Vatican Council (1962–65). As used by Catholics today, liturgy includes not only Sunday Mass but also the church's other sacramental rites and the Liturgy of the Hours (also called the Divine Office).

CHAPTER 1
Sunday Mass: Why Come?

Let's get together!

At the beginning of the semester, I ask my Georgetown University students to name an assembly they have been part of or one they have read about or seen in the news recently. Their lists often include sporting events, concerts, graduation ceremonies, prayer services to remember particular people or events, and rallies to support or protest certain issues. I then ask them, "What brought the people together and how did the experience affect you (or others, if you were not involved personally)?" In response, the students talk about shared ideas or emotions, the need to feel united or supported, and the importance of remembering and celebrating certain occasions in life. They also say that gathering with others makes experiences more meaningful and more memorable. They might even come to feel more enthusiastic about, or more deeply committed to, something.

Generally speaking, people like to get together with one another. It seems to be a basic human instinct to be relational, to want to share our lives with others and to be part of something bigger than ourselves. We are made for relationships and for community: from our faith community to our family, from neighborhoods to workplaces, from the global community to the communion of saints.

What does all this have to do with what we're about at Sunday Mass? First, although the assembling we do for concerts, rallies, or football games is not the same as what we do on Sunday, there are some similarities: (1) as Christians, we identify who we are and believe that this identity is significant; (2) we share certain values to which we can become more deeply committed when we regularly gather together; (3) we can find in the Sunday assembly a sense of unity and support; (4) we celebrate, that is, we *remember* in a very special way. We remember all that God has done and is doing for us in Jesus Christ and in the power of the Holy Spirit. And unlike other kinds of assemblies, the kind of remembering we do on Sunday is not simply recalling past events, but rather, it is a remembering that calls us to attend to God's activity in our lives right now.

Second, that basic instinct we have to want to share our lives, to belong to something, to be in relationship with others . . . well, God knows this about us! In fact, we are made in the image of our Creator, who is *relational*, who shares life with us and invites us into relationship with God and all that God has created. So it's really not surprising that God would call us together as a community to give thanks and praise. And as we will discover later in this book, being part of the Sunday assembly can teach us a lot about how to live in right relationship with God, others, and all of creation.

Why do we come?

Have you ever noticed how much Catholics like processions on Sundays? There's the procession into the church and to our seats, the opening procession, the procession with the Book of the Gospels, the procession with the gifts of wine and bread, the communion rite, and the procession that concludes the celebration and sends us out to love and to serve. When I ask people, "What is the first procession on Sunday?" the most common answer is "the opening procession." But every now and then someone will say with a chuckle, "Getting out of bed!" "That's it!" I say.

What's involved with this first liturgical procession? A decision. There's a choice to make each Sunday (or Saturday afternoon or evening if that is when you choose to go to Mass for that Sunday): to go or not to go to Mass. We have a standing invitation to participate in Sunday worship. Who invites us? God does. God invites, and as with all invitations, a response follows. By choosing to come on Sundays—to be part of the church assembled for worship—we respond positively to God's invitation. It's our first "Amen!" Our first "Yes, so be it!"

Why go to Sunday Mass? Whenever I have asked this question of myself, my answer is never exactly the same. And when I have asked the question of others, they, too, have given many different answers. It strikes me that there isn't simply one good-for-all-people-and-all-times answer to this question. I think the abundance of answers reflects the amazing richness of our Sunday celebrations and of God's activity in our lives.

Still, taking time now and then to reflect on why we go to Sunday Mass can be very helpful; it can give us new insights about our faith journeys. Here are some thoughts from several people in response to the question "Why do you choose to come to Sunday Mass?" Perhaps you can relate to some of their ideas.

- "Gratitude comes first to mind. I come on Sundays to praise and thank God. There's so much to be grateful for—the everyday blessings like my family and my work, the generosity and compassion of so many people, the beauty of nature, just to name a few! I have also learned to be grateful for the difficulties of life, because they lead me to deeper faith."

- "Participating in Sunday Eucharist strengthens and renews my Christian identity. I learn more about who I am and who we are as church."

- "I need the support of the faith community. The people I see gather week after week sustain my faith. I realize that I don't walk alone and that I have good company in my struggles and doubts. I feel very connected to others in the assembly, even if I don't know them personally. We all have something in common: we're all part of the Body of Christ."

- "I suppose I could say that I *have* to come to Mass because it's part of my job as a parish priest, but that's certainly not the only reason. I also come because I need to hear the stories—the stories of Scripture, the church, and my sisters and brothers in Christ. The stories help me *remember* that God is present and active in the world . . . in people's lives . . . in my life!"

- "Sunday Eucharist challenges me. It can make me uncomfortable, which is good! I too easily become complacent, even indifferent to what's going on around me. Participating in Sunday Eucharist wakes me up! I am challenged to do better, to see and to be more concerned about the world, especially its brokenness and need for healing, and to be Christ for others."

- "I come on Sundays ready to be surprised, and I often am! Even though it all seems very familiar, something I hear or see or do often grabs my attention, as though I were experiencing it for the first time. I then ask myself, 'What about that got my attention? What does it mean for my life right now?'"

You are now invited to jot down a few of your own thoughts in response to this question, keeping in mind that our reason for going to Mass might be different from week to week, since each Sunday we bring another week's worth of living.

We are needed!

Have you ever considered that the church—that is, all the baptized— *needs* for us to come to Sunday Mass? Why are we needed?

(1) Coming together on Sundays is a primary way in which the church is visible to the world. Liturgy is public prayer and a place where the church is in the flesh, so to speak. Sunday Mass is a time when we make plain to the world what we are about as a church, a people who share a common baptism and hold common beliefs.

(2) By faithfully gathering on the Lord's Day, the church is able to carry on from one generation to the next, so we have a responsibility to those who will come after us.

(3) There would be no eucharistic celebration without the gathered church. The assembly's participation in this sacramental rite is essential, as we will explore later in this book.

(4) Finally, the Body of Christ is somehow less than it could be when members of the assembly are absent. This was a concern even among the early Christians. A third-century instruction to bishops reads: "When you are teaching, command and exhort the people to be faithful to the assembly of the church. Let them not fail to attend, but let them gather faithfully together. Let no one deprive the church by staying away; if they do,

they deprive the body of Christ of one of its members" *(Didascalia of the Apostles).* Might this understanding apply as much for twenty-first-century Christians as it did for third-century Christians?

Which of the reasons given for why we are needed at Sunday Mass do you relate to? What else would you add to the list?

CHAPTER 2

Sunday Mass:
What Should We Bring?

What should we bring?

Most of us probably don't give much thought to what we bring to Sunday Mass other than practical things like coats on chilly mornings, umbrellas when dark clouds loom, groceries for the parish food pantry, and collection envelopes containing what we are able to give from the fruits of our labors. But what else should we bring? Here are some ideas.

✧ We bring our lives! We bring who we are at that moment and we bring our life "stuff"—the ups and downs, ins and outs of daily living. This probably seems obvious, but some people might squirm at this notion, perhaps out of a sense that the everyday stuff of life is somehow less than holy. Others might feel more comfortable with the idea that they bring their lives to Sunday Mass, yet they really don't know what it is that they bring because they take little time to reflect on what's happening in their lives and how God becomes known in and through their experiences.

What do you think? How does the notion that we bring our ordinary, daily lives to Sunday Mass strike you? In responding to these questions, it might be helpful to recall your last Sunday Mass experience. What "life stuff" did you bring? For example, did you bring any particular worries or struggles? Did you feel distracted by what was on your "to do" list for the week? Were you teeming with joy in the wake of a recent happy occasion? Did you bring your ideals and dreams? Your disappointments and heartaches? Were you looking to make sense of what's going on in your life? Did you come with your depth of prayer and faith? What did you bring?

And what happens with the "life stuff" that you bring to Sunday Mass? For instance, did you find yourself thinking in a new way about something that's going on in your life? Did some of your distractions become less important as you prayed with the assembly? Did words of gratitude come to your lips as you brought to mind the ways in which God was actively present in the day-to-day of your life and the lives of others? Was your hope in your ideals and dreams renewed?

Did you notice that as you named the pieces of daily life that you brought to Sunday Mass, you were also telling your story—at least a small part of it? Recently, my college students had a chance to tell some of their story in a course paper. I asked them what telling their stories did for them. Several said, "It gave me a better understanding of my experiences, and I learned something about myself and the other people involved." Others added, "I could also see where and how God was present, which I didn't realize at the time." I then asked them why it's important to tell our stories and listen to others tell their stories, which led us to talk about how story sharing can begin new relationships and strengthen the ones we already have. And then there are the pearls of wisdom and fresh perspectives that can come both in our telling and in our listening to others. We can also feel a sense of connectedness to a wider human community, realizing that other people have experiences and feelings similar to ours. Finally, one student declared, "Telling my story makes me feel like I matter and my life matters." Yes. Sharing our stories is affirming; it honors the basic goodness and dignity of the persons we are and are becoming.

But what could storytelling possibly have to do with what we should bring to Sunday Mass? For one thing, when we are conscious of our own story and the stories of others with and for whom we pray, we can better understand them in light of our Judeo-Christian story, our story of salvation and of the church, all of which we hear and enact at Sunday Mass. It's somewhat like wanting to know the stories of our families (our living relatives and those who have gone before us); our communities (the towns or cities in which we live, our schools and parishes, for example); our country (whether our home country or the one we have adopted); or our workplaces (namely, the stories of the workers on whose shoulders we now stand). Why do we want to know these stories? I think it's because they are important to understanding our own; they can help us understand better who we are and what place we have in the larger story of the family, the community, the country, or the workplace. We also realize that our stories add to these larger stories, and therefore to the meaning they carry for others.

At Mass we also want to know our place in the larger story of God acting in this world. We realize that our personal stories and the stories of the human community are, in fact, part of the continuing revelation of God in this world. God is actively revealed, that is, made known, in the very "stuff" of our lives. Of course, this doesn't mean that we will ever know God fully, for God is Mystery; yet, at the same time, God is intimately involved in people's lives, so we and others can come to know God better by paying attention to what is happening in our lives.

✧ "I come filled with expectation!" she announced. "Every Sunday, no matter my mood, no matter what is weighing on my mind, I imagine myself sitting on the edge of my seat. I'll tell you why I do this," she continued, "because I discovered a long time ago that if I don't come to Mass wanting something to happen, little will change in me or in my life—or for that matter, in the church, since it's about more than just me." Stirring words from a seventy-something lifelong Catholic. Notice what this woman brings to liturgy: an expectant mindset, an eagerness, a readiness. She is open to something happening and to the possibility that it could change not only her life but that of the faith community.

This is probably not something that most of us have thought about, maybe because liturgy can seem rather predictable. We know it—at least we think we do. Yes, by its very nature the ritual we call Mass is repetitive, and it can seem more or less the same week after week. But is it really? We might need to look again, while sitting "on the edge of our seats." Do we go to Sunday Mass wanting to do or hear or see or taste or smell or feel something that might change us? Are we open to the possibility of change in our hearts, in how we live, in how we are church? And if we're not, what is keeping us from being receptive to the possibility that our experience might very well invite change?

Do you come to Mass expectant? What difference does or could it make to be "on the edge of your seat," open to something happening that might change you—and us?

_____

_____

_____

_____

_____

_____

✧ Do we bring intentionality or a mindfulness when we come for Mass? If you're like me, there are moments in the day when you're on autopilot or in daydream mode. Maybe it's during your morning routine, your commute to work or school, or your daily household chores. It's those times when we go through the motions but aren't all that present to what we're doing. We might also be terrific multitaskers. We can, for example, talk on the phone, do e-mail, watch TV, and surf the Internet all at the same time. Many of us can multitask with ease, but do we really attend to any single thing or, even more importantly, to any single person?

It's not surprising that the multitasker, autopilot, and daydreamer come along when we go to Sunday liturgy. I know that I sometimes catch my multitasking self placing my fingers in the holy water font, signing myself, greeting people, and grabbing a worship aid in what seems to be one motion and without much conscious thought. My autopilot then takes over as I walk up the aisle and sit in my "usual" place. How present, how aware am I to what I am doing, to what is happening, to the community as it gathers to praise and thank God? After all, it is here and now as the people assemble that our worship begins. *And,* how present am I to the presence of Christ, for *Christ is present* when the church gathers to pray and sing?

How might we get into the habit of bringing our intentionality and presence of mind and heart with us on Sundays? I have learned that it requires practice—discipline, really. When we arrive at the church doors, about to cross the threshold into our prayer together, we might learn to call to mind *whom* we celebrate—Jesus Christ. We might remind ourselves, "Here and now, in this gathering, Christ is present, actively working and praying in and with and through us." Christ is actively present. Are we?

Presence. What does it mean for us to be present to others and to what we do in our day-to-day lives? What does it mean to you when someone is present to you? Tell about experiences you have had of being present, actively present, to another person, as well as when someone was really present to you. How would these experiences have been different if you or the other person had been distracted or inattentive?

Our everyday experiences of presence—of being intentional about what we say and do, about how we look and listen—point to the importance of bringing this same sensibility to Sunday Mass. And might it also be that the Mass has something to teach us about paying deeper attention to the day-to-day occurrences of our lives—to who crosses our path of life, to what is happening in the world near and far, and to the movements within our own hearts? Could our presence to who and what we encounter during Sunday Eucharist help us to be more mindful of Christ's presence not only at Mass but in our midst as we go about living our lives?

What do you think? Does being actively present to what is happening during Mass make a difference (a) in how you experience the liturgy and (b) in how you relate to others and go about doing what you do the rest of the week?

_____

_____

_____

_____

_____

What helps you to be mindful about what you are doing and saying when you come to Mass? What gets in the way?

_____

_____

_____

_____

Try this: The next time you go to Sunday Mass, become conscious of the presence of Christ as the people are gathering. You might even offer a prayer such as: "Here we are, Lord Jesus. Your church gathered. You present to us. Help us to be present to you." Does this awareness of the presence of Christ in the assembly affect your experience of the liturgy? If so, how?

_____

_____

_____

_____

✧ *"Can you imagine?"* A friend who is a Benedictine priest in Uganda, East Africa, likes to punctuate his stories with this question, a question that also reveals something about him. My friend approaches life with imagination—not some sort of fantasizing that is out of touch with the realities of this world, but rather the ability to see more than the obvious and imagine what's possible. In fact, he has a strong *sacramental imagination,* meaning that he practices seeing the potential of God being revealed in everyone and everything. I think this is what enables him to envision what's possible—that which might not be obvious at first but which can become the new reality because there is something of God in it all.

Imagination is a gift each of us has. We might say that we are "hard-wired" to be able to imagine. Thank goodness. Think of the many ways in which we use our imaginations every day: maintaining relationships with family and friends, raising children, creating a home, doing our jobs and our homework, enjoying hobbies, playing a musical instrument, listening to favorite tunes on our iPods, reading newspapers and novels, inventing new things, finding new ways to do something, telling stories, making decisions, addressing humanitarian crises and social injustices, just to name a few! Our imaginations help us to find meaning in life and come to *know* God, ourselves, and others in new and deeper ways.

And what if we stir into our natural ability to imagine a sacramental outlook? As Catholics, sacramentality is in our bones; it shapes our attitudes, actions, and prayer. A sacramental "take" on life means that we can recognize the extraordinary splendor of God in ordinary people and experiences. It's the lens that helps us to see more than meets the eye, the aid that enables us to hear in new ways, the filter that directs our thoughts and actions. Ultimately, I believe, a sacramental imagination can help us do our part in reshaping the world.

Where do we get this special way of imagining? For one thing, it seeps into us as we participate in the Sunday assembly. Sunday Eucharist is certainly a primary time and place for our imagination to be stretched and to take on a sacramental quality. How does this happen? I think we will discover as we continue our exploration of the Sunday assembly that it happens when what we bring—our lives and expectant mindset, our presence and the gift of human imagination—meets the many sights, sounds, smells, words, and actions of the eucharistic celebration. What might seem so ordinary takes on extraordinary meaning as we participate in the work of Christ. We practice recognizing in everyday life the potential of God being made known to us. We use our sacramental imagination.

Are you in touch with the power of your imagination? Name some of the many ways you use your imagination in living your life.

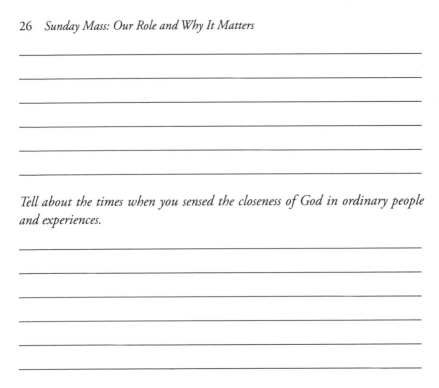

Tell about the times when you sensed the closeness of God in ordinary people and experiences.

❖ "I used to think of Sunday Mass as a kind of escape. I mean there's just always so much going on in my own life, and then I am bombarded by the many crises and needs in the world. I thought of Mass as a time to shut it all out." Maybe all of us at times have felt as this fifty-year-old business owner did, but as we will see in chapter 5, our gathering for Sunday Mass and the needs of the world are tightly bound up together.

This points to the last idea for what we should bring to Sunday Eucharist: a concern for the world near and far, from our homes to our workplaces and schools, from our neighborhoods to our nation, from our local communities to the global community. Every Sunday we are asked to pray for the church, for local needs, and for the world. In fact, as Christians we celebrate the Eucharist for the salvation of the church and the world, that is, we participate in this sacred event so that we and the entire church and all that the Gracious Mystery has created and is creating may live out of the gift of relationship with God. To do this, I think it's important to be aware of the needs of the church and the world to respond to those needs.

I asked the business owner what he meant when he said that he "used to" think of Sunday Mass as a time to shut the world out. He said:

> I learned something along the way. It was after the September 11, 2001, terrorist attacks in the U.S. People flocked to churches to pray. I remember the

Sunday Masses at my parish were packed for several weeks. I also remember how more tuned in I was to our prayers for the world. I just never really paid attention to this before. I realized for the first time that the Eucharist is for the world and that we can't celebrate the Eucharist unconcerned. I don't think we need to know every detail of every situation that calls for our attention. That's not possible. But I learned that by being generally concerned about the world, I listen differently, I pray differently. It's risky, because as I have come to bring a concern for the world to Mass, my heart has expanded and I feel I must do more to help people in need.

CHAPTER 3

The Sunday Assembly:
Who *Are* All These People?

Who *are* all these people?

Now that we have thought about why we come to Sunday Mass and have talked about what we bring with us, our next question as we look around the church might be "Who *are* all these people?" There is more than one answer to this question, because as we will see, there is more than one way to speak about the Sunday assembly.

We're a mixed bunch!

The writer James Joyce once described Catholicism as "Here comes everybody!" We need only picture in our mind's eye for a moment the faces we see at Sunday Mass to know that Joyce was right-on. The diversity of the Sunday assembly is awe-inspiring. We are a marvelous assortment of people. We come in all ages—from the newborn to the elderly. We are married, single, divorced, widowed, lay and ordained. We bring a rich variety of ethnic, cultural, and educational backgrounds. We call different places home and speak many languages. Some of us are students; most of us are workers—in our homes, on the job, and in the community. We are the well-to-do, the barely-making-ends-meet, and everything in-between. Some of us bring health concerns or other worries. We have varying interests and commitments, likes and dislikes. We are of different political leanings and have various approaches to church and societal matters. "Here comes everybody" indeed!

All these differences, and yet we are so much alike. We all need to love and to be loved. We want to make sense out of life and to know that we matter. We know the pull of the Spirit and the need for God and one another. And as the baptized, we share a common name and identity in Christ.

Imagine that! Each of us is a unique person, all of us together a "mixed bunch," bonded by the same human needs and united by our baptism in Christ. The Sunday assembly—at one with Christ and with people, some of whom we know, others whom we have never met. Where else do we experience this kind of phenomenon?

"Here comes everybody!" Who makes up the Sunday assembly at your parish? Take a few minutes to talk about your diversity and your sameness.

———————————————————————————

———————————————————————————

———————————————————————————

———————————————————————————

———————————————————————————

———————————————————————————

How does the assembly's diversity and at the same time its oneness in Christ affect your own experience of Sunday Eucharist?

———————————————————————————

———————————————————————————

———————————————————————————

———————————————————————————

———————————————————————————

———————————————————————————

We are a community of remembering

Remembering has much to do with why Christians come together to worship on Sundays. In fact, we have a special word for the kind of remembering that we do—*anamnesis*. It's a Greek word that means "remembrance" or "calling to mind," and yet it is more than this. The kind of remembering we do on Sundays is not simply recalling past events, but rather we remember that Christ is really present and active here and now in our gathering and in our lives.

Of course, we human beings can be very forgetful, and not simply in the sense of forgetting where we put our car keys or forgetting what it is we wanted in another room once we arrived there. We can be forgetful about turning toward God in our daily choices. We can be forgetful about being there for someone who needs us. We can be forgetful about seeing Christ in the faces of the poor and the unemployed, the homeless and the hungry, the abused and the neglected, the lonely and the grieving, the sick and the dying. We can be forgetful about being grateful for all God has done and is doing for us.

Sunday Eucharist helps us remember all of what we can so easily forget. There are special memory aids for us at Mass; they are the symbols and rituals, the prayers and songs, the Scripture readings and homily. We also have one another! I like to think of the people who surround me in the Sunday assembly as my memory partners. They help me remember why I am there and remind me of who I am and am called to be as a Christian. Their being there, their participation in the words and actions, their faith, and their remembering all that God has done and is doing for us are my memory aids. We are what Christians have always been: a community of remembering.

How might being part of the assembly every Sunday help you to remember who you are and are called to be as a Christian?

_____

_____

_____

_____

_____

_____

We are the Body of Christ

I once conducted a day of retreat in a parish where the Sunday assembly was invited to greet one another before the entrance procession and opening song. Knowing this, I said to this group gathered there, "Pretend you have just been told to introduce yourselves to one another at Mass and say, 'Hello. I'm the Body of Christ.'" A moment's hesitation. A ripple of laughter. Then it began—many with broad smiles, others feeling unsure, everyone shaking hands and saying, "Hello. I'm the Body of Christ." "How did saying your common name feel?" I asked. "Uncomfortable." "Something I never thought about." "Pretty amazing." "It's quite a name to live up to, isn't it?"

I wonder whether the early Christians to whom St. Paul wrote had similar reactions. He is believed to have been the first New Testament writer to speak about the assembly of the baptized as the Body of Christ, with Christ as "the head of the body" (Colossians 1:18). As people baptized in Christ, we are a new creation, the Body of Christ (see 2 Corinthians 5:17). Paul's words also remind us that the Christian assembly is Christ's work. Christ leads us; we are invited to respond.

Unfortunately, the early Christians' self-understanding as the Body of Christ was overlooked for several centuries. The good news is that this way of speaking about the Christian assembly captured the imagination of the Second Vatican Council (1962–65), which reintroduced this essential identity to the church. For example, the Council's *Constitution on the Sacred Liturgy* reads: "In [liturgy] full public worship is performed by the Mystical Body of Jesus Christ, that is, by the head and its members" (no. 7). "Body of Christ" is truly quite a name to live up to when we gather for Eucharist and as we live in this world.

Living up to our name . . . We are reminded of our name every time we receive Communion. The Communion minister names the consecrated bread and wine and names us: "The Body of Christ," "The Blood of Christ." We say "Amen." What does it mean to us at Mass and after Mass to say "Amen" (meaning "So be it") to this name of ours?

_____

_____

_____

_____

_____

We are the church

Back to St. Paul for a moment. When Paul spoke about the baptized as the Body of Christ, he also named this Body "the church": Christ is "the head of the body, the church" (Colossians 1:18). Paul also says that the church, as Christ's Body, is "the fullness of the one who fills all things in every way" (Ephesians 1:22-23). We, as the Body of Christ, as the church, are a visible sign of Christ's presence in this world. We become especially visible when we gather for Eucharist. It's as though someone could look in on us and say, "There's the church at prayer."

And what does that someone see? Like a mirror, we reflect who the church is and is becoming when we come together for Eucharist. In looking at the Sunday assembly, it is clear that the church is, as we discussed earlier, a "mixed bunch," a wonderful assortment of people united by baptism. The church is also holy and sinful, graced but always in need of conversion. We strive to live in right relationship with God and with others, but there are times when we turn away and even do harm to our relationships. We have moments of greatness and moments of failure. We are often self-giving but sometimes self-centered. We are forgiving but also in need of forgiveness. The church is wounded, sometimes divided; we are fragile yet steadfast. In other words, everything we are, the church is too.

Once, when I mentioned the idea that we are the church, the Body of Christ, to a group of liturgical ministers at a small rural parish, a middle-aged man eagerly told his story about imagining the people he saw on Sundays as the church and Body of Christ:

> A few years ago, I heard someone else say what you're saying, so I decided one Sunday to get to church early and take a good look at everyone who came. Of course, since I live in a small town, everyone looked familiar. I knew many of them. They were my relatives, neighbors, friends, and co-workers. I saw the teachers from the local school, my children's friends and their families. There were the community leaders and local business people. I saw people I like and people I don't like. As I watched everyone, I said to myself, "*This* is the church? *We* are the Body of Christ?" We just all seemed so ordinary, and we certainly aren't perfect. But I began to sense that there is something more to it. I remembered that line from one of the Gospels where Jesus said, "Where two or more are gathered, there am I." I realized that what makes us something more is that Christ is there. And so to see these very familiar people as the church and the Body of Christ was suddenly something very real. Still, it's really rather a mystery to me.

I was impressed by what this man did and by the insights he offered about his experience. He certainly exercised his sacramental imagination, didn't he? He looked at the ordinary people of the Sunday assembly and recognized the extraordinary. He was able to see the presence of Christ, which enabled him to see those people who were so familiar to him in a new way, that is, as the church, as the Body of Christ. This man also spoke of this experience as mystery, and by that I don't think he meant that he had absolutely no understanding about it. He did have understanding, but he also sensed that this mystery of the church as the baptized members of the Body of Christ cannot be fully understood. After all, we gather to praise God, who is both known and unknown to us.

Can you imagine? Have you ever taken a good look at the people who come together for Sunday Mass at your parish? Can you see in them the church, the Body of Christ? How might seeing them in this way influence your experience of the Mass?

_____

_____

_____

_____

_____

We are symbol and sacrament

The news report was about a tragic fire that claimed the lives of over a hundred people. The reporter narrated the events unfolding before him, which included a spontaneous prayer vigil and creation of a makeshift memorial to honor those who had died. Grief-stricken people gathered at the site, many with candles in hand, others with flowers, some bearing special mementos of their now deceased loved ones. I was struck by the reporter's concluding words: "People seem to need their symbols."

We do need symbols, don't we? Why? To answer this, it might be helpful to think about a few common symbols: a wedding ring, a nation's flag, memorials concerning people or events, art and poetry, songs and mottos, a salute or an embrace, standing for a national anthem at a ballgame, fasting in support of the hungry. Each of us can certainly add to this list, because regardless of how conscious we are of it, symbols are a key aspect of living.

What do symbols do for us? Our instincts tell us that they help us get beneath the surface of our experiences and find meaning. For example, a wedding ring is more than a gold band with a diamond setting; it speaks of love and fidelity. A nation's flag is more than colorful fabrics stitched together; it expresses a history and certain common values. Memorials are more than slabs of concrete; they invite us to remember someone or something here and now. We're not just stretching our legs when we stand for a national anthem; we're showing respect and unity with others.

Symbols put us in touch with our deepest feelings and give us ways to express them, especially when words alone aren't enough. Symbols also offer many layers of meaning, so what a work of art or a pressed flower in a book means to you might mean something different to me. And one symbol can carry many meanings for the same person. For example, I wear a ring that has the diamonds from my mother's wedding band. When I look at or feel the ring, I know my mother's love in giving it to me, the grace of my parents' marriage, and my place in the family. Also, my dad, who died when I was a teen, is very present to me. Many symbols also cross generational and cultural lines, because people of all ages and backgrounds can find meaning in them.

So, yes, we do need our symbols. They can seem ever so ordinary, but they become extraordinary because, in a very real sense, they put us in touch with our deeper selves and invite us to participate in our life experiences in meaningful ways. In fact, symbols can change us if we absorb the new insights they offer.

Religious symbols do all that nonreligious symbols do and more. Through seemingly ordinary actions, words, and objects that we can experience with our senses, the Mystery of God is made real for us. Our participation in these symbols leads us to encounter the Holy One, which can change us. Extraordinary.

Christian worship is packed with symbols. Think, for example, of Sunday Mass, where we are wrapped in symbols—gestures, words, actions, objects, *and* people. "People as symbols?" you ask. Yes, but I am going to keep you curious for a brief time while we take a quick look at the other kinds of liturgical symbols. In chapter 4 we'll spend a little more time on how we participate in these symbols, so a warm-up exercise here will prepare us for our later work.

Since we regularly experience the abundant symbols of our Eucharist, list the liturgical symbols that come to mind and speak about what they say to you. How do they help you to experience the Sacred?

Some ideas from a few others might be helpful in getting started:

- "The first symbol that comes to mind is the one I see first when I walk into church—our beautiful baptismal pool. Dipping my fingers into the pool and making the sign of the cross remind me that I am a baptized person and part of what will happen as I celebrate Eucharist with everyone."

- "The Book of the Gospels. As a deacon, it is my privilege to carry this book into the church and to proclaim the gospel from it. I am very aware of Christ present in our midst at these moments. It's very moving."

- "I love the music—the songs we sing and the music that's played while we pray silently. The words are like poetry, and although we sing many familiar songs, there's always something new that I hear, something that helps me understand better how I am to live as a Christian. And the instrumental pieces take my breath away at times. I feel a real closeness to God and to everyone around me."

- "I bow deeply before the altar before I move into my usual row of seats. The altar is the symbol of Christ, so bowing gives me a focus for the Mass. I am reminded that Christ is present right now, right here."

- "The sign of peace is the symbol that stands out for me. When I hear 'Peace of Christ' from people I don't even know, I feel a connection with them, and I think of the great need for peace in our world."

Your turn. What symbols stand out for you and why?

_____

_____

_____

_____

_____

_____

Now back to people, the assembly, as liturgical symbol. We have already hinted rather strongly at this idea when we talked about the assembly as the Body of Christ and as the church. These names we have are symbolic. They express in powerful images that which escapes long-winded explanations—our intimate union with Christ and one another in the Body of Christ, and our responsibility to make Christ's presence known to the world by being the church we are. We can also say, then, that the assembly is a symbol of Christ's presence at Mass and in the world. Ordinary people who, because we gather in Christ's name, become something even more—an encounter with the real presence of Christ.

What else can we say about the assembly as symbol? When I look at the faces of the Sunday assembly in my parish, I see hope and possibility. I think the fact that we twenty-first-century Christians continue to gather to celebrate the Eucharist on Sundays says that we are a symbol of God's ongoing activity in the world. It's as though our assembling and sharing the Eucharist announce to a world in need of Easter hope: "Never give up! God continues to be intimately involved in human life, and everything is possible for God."

A woman who was one of the founding members of her parish some forty years ago shared what she has noticed about the people who come to Sunday Mass:

> I sometimes look at the faces in church on Sunday and think about how often they seem to change. The children I once knew are parents of the infants and children I have yet to meet. People move in and out of the parish, as jobs bring them here and take them away. Many faces are aging—like mine. And of course, I think of the parishioners who are now celebrating in heaven. They are absent faces on Sunday but somehow never far away in spirit.

I think this woman's story reflects yet another dimension of the Sunday assembly. We are a symbol of the human journey, our pilgrimage on earth and our looking toward what is to come. The assembly reminds us that God's reign is here and now and to come.

On a final note, in the fifth century St. Augustine gave us a way of understanding what a sacrament is, and the church still uses his definition. He spoke about a sacrament as "a visible sign of an invisible grace." In essence, all we have been saying about the assembly as symbol is also to say that the assembly is sacrament. As flesh and bones, heart, soul and mind, we are a visible sign of the gift of God's Self to the world.

Symbols can often invite us to change, because they can lead us to know ourselves better and to open us up to new ways of thinking and acting. In what ways might the symbol of the Sunday assembly invite us to change?

CHAPTER 4

The Sunday Assembly: We Have Work to Do

Liturgy is work

I mentioned in the Introduction that the word "liturgy" comes from the Greek word *leitourgia,* which, roughly translated, means "the work of the people." When speaking about the church's worship in particular, it's more accurate to say that liturgy is God working in and through the work of the people. Thus we share in God's work, which the Spirit of Christ enables us to do. Of course, as with any meaningful work, this means it's important to show up and do more than simply put in the time. In order to contribute to the work of celebrating Sunday Eucharist, we need to be actively present. This is work we agreed to do by virtue of our baptismal promises, to which we say "Amen—So be it" every time we participate in the Eucharist.

What is the assembly's work?

This chapter might more properly be entitled "We have *more* work to do," since our work begins long before we stand for the opening song at Mass. As we learned earlier, living our lives as Christian people is an essential part of our work. Our work continues when we make the decision to gather with and as the church on Sunday. Bringing our stories, coming expectant and being *actively* present, exercising our sacramental imagination, and being concerned about the world—all this is our work as the eucharistic assembly. It is also our work to pay attention to who we are, rejoicing in our diversity and our unity and living up to our names as the Body of Christ and the church, and serving as a visible symbol of God's life-giving love for all God has created.

As we recap these pieces of the assembly's work, an important theme emerges that I think will guide us as we explore even more facets of our work. Have you ever been asked what your work in life is—in one sentence or less? Many of us have probably been asked this during small talk at a social function or perhaps on some printed form with barely enough space in which to describe our work. What would you say if you were asked in similar fashion to describe the work we do as the Sunday assembly? I would say "to be present and active." Our work as active presence—this is an idea to keep before us as we continue our exploration of the many facets of the assembly's work.

Our work as ministry

"Sign-up Sunday" is a common yearly event in many parishes. Parishioners are invited to sign up for various activities, including liturgical ministries for Sunday Mass: lector, eucharistic minister, cantor, choir member, musician, greeter, usher, sacristan, and acolyte or server. And, of course, there are liturgical ministries that those called to ordination fulfill, namely, the roles of the presiding priest and assisting deacon. However, before the community calls any of us to serve in these particular ministries, we must first be enrolled in the liturgical ministry that is even more fundamental to all eucharistic celebrations. But we won't find a sign up sheet for this important liturgical ministry because we're already signed up—all of us! Baptism gives us our first and most basic liturgical ministry: *to be the assembly.*

It might be useful to think about what we mean by "ministry," since it's such a common word in our church and in society. What comes to mind? I think first about what we know from the Gospels about Jesus' ministry, which was characterized by giving of self, being present to and serving others, receiving the service of others, building up relationships, and inviting people to turn toward God. The ways of ministry that Jesus modeled for us were always in the service of spreading the Good News and working to make the world more like God intended it to be.

If you accept these notions about ministry, the next question is: "How, as the Sunday Mass assembly, do we give of ourselves, serve others, receive what others give us, build up relationships, and do our part in inviting people into deeper relationship with God?" It strikes me that there is no hard and fast list of ways in which we do all of this. There are many possibilities that come to light, depending on the makeup and needs of the assembly.

This might all be a bit overwhelming to us at first. I ask myself, for example, "Am I up to this?" My answer to this question is, first, I find courage in knowing that none of us goes it alone. The Holy Spirit is actively working in and through us as individuals and as the assembly. And as an assembly, we have each other to look to and lean on; in other words, the ministry of being the eucharistic assembly is a shared responsibility. Second, I think we can trust that through our baptism, the gift of faith, and a life of prayer, God has given us what we need to grow into our ministry and do it well.

Before we go on to consider what might be on the list of ways that the Sunday Mass assembly carries out its ministry, let's pause to reflect on what's been said so far about our Sunday work as ministry. What are your thoughts? What questions are raised for you?

_____

_____

_____

_____

_____

_____

Carrying out our ministry as assembly

Once again, there is no exhaustive list of the ways in which we as the assembly do the work of ministry. Mass is a living celebration that real people who bring the real stuff of life take part in, so the assembly's ministry must also be active and responsive to the changing needs of the gathered church. For our purposes here, I will offer four ways in which we carry out our ministry as a eucharistic assembly.

Being actively present

The first way to minister is already familiar to us, and it points directly to that guiding theme I suggested earlier. In chapter 2 we talked about the importance of bringing a mindfulness and a presence to Sunday Eucharist. We thought about the possible impact on our experience of Mass if we are present, *actively* present, to Christ's presence, to one another, and to the action of the liturgy. How is this also part of our ministry? What comes to mind is how right it feels when someone is actively present to me and I am present in the same way to others. I also know from my own Mass experiences that when the assembly is mindful and actively present to the presence of Christ and to what is happening, I am also more likely to be. So if ministry is about giving of ourselves, being for and receiving others, and inviting one another to become more and more aware of the always available gift of God in our lives, then being actively present at Sunday Mass is indeed ministry.

Offering the gift of hospitality

The word "hospitality" brings various images to mind: "Hi, how are you?" when we meet up with someone; a hotel hospitality suite, where guests may go for beverages and snacks; a social club's hospitality committee, charged with providing refreshments for meetings; the hospitality we offer people who come to our homes; and the particular hospitality ministries in many parishes, such as ushers and greeters. Do you notice the common elements underlying these examples of hospitality? Greeting and welcoming, receiving and being received, serving and being served, keeping up relationships we have and discovering new ones, and feasting with special food and drink. Hospitality is full of life! We invest a great deal of ourselves in this human activity. And it *is* activity, engaging us and inviting our participation in whatever is happening.

Oftentimes our everyday experiences of hospitality are also experiences of *Christian* hospitality. What is hospitality with a Christian flair? Think for a moment about people you know whom you describe as being "all heart" or having a "big heart." What is it about them that makes you say this? Maybe it's that they regularly give of themselves and do so without hesitation and without expecting anything in return. We might also say that they have the habit of presence, which communicates a generosity and sensitivity and makes people feel accepted. To me, these habits of the heart speak to what hospitality means for Christians. We are asked to have an expansive heart, one that can make room for everyone.

Have you ever been the stranger in the room, the person other people mistrust, don't recognize, or may even avoid? Or have you had some other experience of being an outsider, unsure of whether you belong, or the foreigner without a claim to the place you are visiting? Do you know or can you imagine what it's like to be displaced from your home, to be a refugee, a wanderer, or an immigrant looking for open arms? If your answer is yes to any of these questions, you know how hard it can be to be the stranger and how someone's welcome can change everything. We also know it's not easy to welcome the stranger. It can feel risky, because we don't know what to expect when we reach out to someone we don't know. Yet this, too, is part of the hard work of Christian hospitality.

Jesus actively welcomed strangers, and we see in the gospel stories that his welcome changed everything for them and often for the bystanders. Strangers were visible to Jesus; they were named and included, forgiven and healed, invited into relationship with him and others. Welcoming *everyone* was essential to Jesus' mission, and as such, to Christian discipleship. It takes courage to welcome the stranger, but a welcome really can change everything.

Finally, what is said about Christian hospitality in chapter 53 of the ancient Rule of St. Benedict is also especially meaningful: "All guests who present themselves are to be welcomed as Christ, for he himself will say: I was a stranger and you welcomed me (Matthew 25:35)." Imagine the possibilities when we receive another as we would Christ.

Describe experiences of giving and receiving Christian hospitality in your life. Do any of these strike you now as moments of ministry? As encounters with Christ? As times when the hospitality offered changed everything?

_____

_____

_____

_____

_____

_____

I was in my early twenties when I moved to Toledo, Ohio. I remember well the first Mass I attended at the nearby Catholic Church, St. Patrick of Heatherdowns. In his homily the priest mentioned the parish population, which was about nine times greater than my entire hometown! I swallowed hard as I looked at the more than a few hundred faces of the assembly. "I'm not sure there's room for me here," I thought. But then something drew me in and kept me coming back for the next thirteen years, and that was a genuine hospitality. I was a stranger, but the welcome mat was out. The moment I sheepishly walked through the door, I was greeted with a smile and a "Good morning" from the person handing out the hymnals. The assembly's active participation in the Mass invited *my* participation, allowing me to feel part of a community that I was meeting for the first time. I also detected a "big heart" in their way of being for and toward one another, which spilled over into other parish activities and outreach efforts. They probably were not even conscious of it, but the assembly at this suburban parish was a true minister of hospitality. There was room for me, after all.

I soon learned that this parish made room for many others. One morning when I arrived at the church, I saw a stranger pacing back and forth in the gathering space. His shabby appearance and odd behavior made me uncomfortable; I froze and was unable to reach out to this gentleman. Thankfully, two parishioners who also came for liturgy that morning were not frozen in fear. They were actively present. They welcomed the stranger and invited him to go with them, first for breakfast and then to a place where he was given the care he needed. The hospitality they offered the stranger in our midst was extraordinary and made a difference not only for the stranger but for many of us in the assembly. The experience changed all of us to some degree. Even that very day the assembly seemed more present to one another as we prayed. And as you might expect, the hospitality we witnessed challenged us to be just as courageous in reaching out to someone in need.

What do you notice about the hospitality of the Sunday assembly at your parish? In what ways is this important aspect of the assembly's liturgical ministry expressed? Some questions might prompt your reflection:

- Do we, the members of the assembly, greet and welcome one another?

- Do we have a sense of what's happening in one another's lives, be it joys, difficulties, sickness, grief, worries, confusion, uncertainty, or exciting new adventures?

- Are we close enough to know who is not there, including the sick and homebound, the Sunday worker and traveler, and those who stay away because they feel excluded or unwelcome?

- Are we concerned about what is happening in the world?

- Do we have a "big heart"?

- How is everyone welcomed and included—the stranger, the outsider, the marginalized, the neglected, and even those whom society rejects?

- Are we welcoming as Christ was welcoming?

- Does our involvement in the action of the Mass inspire participation in the celebration?

_____

_____

_____

_____

_____

_____

Helping one another to remember

This way of carrying out our ministry as assembly is also already familiar to us. Remembering all that God has done and is doing through Jesus Christ and the indwelling of the Holy Spirit is the reason we gather on Sundays. At the same time, although we come together for Mass *because* we remember, we also come together *in order* to remember. In other words, as we mentioned in chapter 3, our eucharistic celebrations themselves remind us of why we gather. Encountering the many symbols, for example, helps us to remember. As a key symbol, the assembly helps us to remember. Praying as one body, united in Christ by our baptism, we are prompted to remember and give thanks to God for promises fulfilled.

But how is this ministry? To help answer this question and better appreciate the remembering we do as a eucharistic assembly, I invite you first to talk about other experiences of remembering.

Recall a recent experience you have had of remembering certain people and/or events. Were other people involved in this occasion of remembering? If so, what do you think remembering with others added to the experience, or how might the experience have been different if you had done the remembering alone?

_____

_____

_____

_____

_____

How did the remembering happen on these occasions? For example, did people tell stories? Did anyone pull out a photo album or other keepsakes? Was there singing, or was something in particular read? Was a meal shared or some special food prepared?

_____

_____

_____

_____

_____

_____

What did the remembering do to you and/or the other people? For instance . . .

- If you were remembering a person, maybe you could sense his/her presence.

- If you told stories about a significant event, emotions similar to what you experienced at the time might have welled up.

- The remembering might have affected relationships. Were any relationships changed? Did new relationships come about, perhaps because the remembering made you feel close to someone you didn't know until then? Were any broken relationships healed because the remembering moved people to forgiveness?

- Maybe the occasion of remembering with others brought about new insights or helped people find new meaning.

- Did the remembering give people a greater sense of identity as a family, school, nation, or global community, for example?

- Did people point to how God was actively present in the person or time remembered?

_____

_____

_____

_____

_____

_____

Did you notice as you shared your experiences that the remembering we do is often about more than the past? The "now" and maybe even the "yet to come" are also involved: the remembering makes a person or event present to us, relationships are formed or changed, new insights or meanings come to light, identity is strengthened, the work of God is recognized.

Did you also notice that the remembering we do with other people calls for an active presence? If we are really present to the people gathered and the occasion, and actively engaged in the remembering by telling stories, listening, singing, and so on, the remembering can take hold of us, maybe even change us.

I believe that our ordinary experiences of remembering tell us a great deal about our ministry of helping one another remember when we gather to celebrate Eucharist. For example, as is often the case on other occasions, we don't remember alone at Mass; we remember as an assembly, which binds us together, strengthens our remembering, and affirms our identity.

As with the experiences of remembering discussed above, the remembering we do on Sundays is about more than the past. The "now" and the "yet to come" are always involved, as the remembering we do at Mass can give new meaning to what's happening in our lives, shape our attitudes, change relationships, direct us in building up God's reign in the world, and point us to the heavenly banquet.

Our Sunday remembering also calls for the assembly to be actively present. The remembering can take hold of us when we are consciously engaged in the assembly's remembering. How do we do this? By offering our lives and our baptismal promise to live in relationship with God; to live up to our name, the Body of Christ; to be church, a visible sign of God's presence in the world. We also proclaim, preach on, and listen to the sacred stories from Scripture, recalling our common story of salvation. We use certain objects, like water, bread, wine, oils, and candles, and we sing and pray special words, all of which can draw us into the remembering. We share a sacred meal, one that nourishes us for the work we are sent to do here and now as the baptized. And in our remembering before God, we invite one another to turn toward Christ, who is actively present in our celebration. Helping one another do this important work of remembering is truly ministry.

Teaching one another to pray

When I was a young girl, I often went to the early Sunday morning Mass with my dad. I loved going to Mass with him, and it wasn't just because we usually would then go home and make pancakes for the rest of the family. As I reflect now on why I cherished those Sunday mornings in church with my dad, I realize that there was something about the way he prayed that captured my imagination. I remember watching him during Mass. I noticed how he actively paid attention and took part in the liturgy. He listened thoughtfully; he joined his voice to the other voices in responding in word and song; he was sincere in his actions, from the sign of the cross to the sign of peace. You might say he *prayed well*. And even as a child, I could somehow sense that his prayer was authentic, perhaps because I could also sense it in how he prayed outside of Mass and how he lived his life.

Praying alongside my dad, joining my voice to his and to those of the other members of the assembly, I learned a great deal about prayer. The learning, however, goes on. I continue to learn about prayer from the people I pray with every time I participate in a eucharistic celebration, and I hope they learn something from me as well. I believe we as the assembly have much to learn from one another about what it means to be people who pray. For instance, we learn that prayer keeps us looking to God and increases our awareness of the world's needs; that it can both console and challenge us; that we sometimes struggle to pray, but that we need to keep doing it anyway; and that prayer can change us.

What have you learned about prayer from the people you pray with at Eucharist?

_____

_____

_____

_____

_____

_____

I said above that my dad prayed well. There is tremendous value in our praying well as members of the Sunday assembly. In fact, I believe it is one of those ways in which we carry out our work of ministry, since praying requires that we offer something of ourselves, that we are open to receiving what others give as they pray, and that our prayer together is always in the service of spreading the Good News and inviting one another and the world to turn toward God. But what does it mean to "pray well" and why is it important that we carry out the ministry of helping the church pray well at Sunday Eucharist?

Once again, because eucharistic assemblies are wonderfully diverse and liturgy is never the same experience from Sunday to Sunday, I can suggest here only a few ideas about what it means to pray well. You will no doubt be able to add to the list. Authenticity comes first to mind. When I am part of an assembly that is praying well, I cannot help but feel that we believe what we are saying and doing. There is a realness to the praying that one could almost reach out and touch. Along with this is a sense that we believe in one another and that we trust our prayer together.

At the same time, this doesn't mean that we always believe what we are saying and doing. There might be times when we are uncertain, when we come filled with nothing but doubt. Maybe we even feel that we can't pray. After a workplace accident claimed her thirty-year-old son's life, a grieving mother said she went to Mass Sunday after Sunday, but she could not pray: "I was filled with so much grief that I could not even pray about my own loss. And I certainly could not pray for others or for the needs of the church or the world. The only words that came to mind were 'God, please receive the prayers of this assembly as my own.'" Many of us have probably known such times, but as members of a praying assembly, we can lean on the prayers of the gathered church. And, of course, at other times we know that others might need to lean on us. Praying well is a shared responsibility.

Returning to our theme of active presence, praying well also means that we are really there and actively participating. We might check ourselves: how intentional are we with our gestures and movements? For example, do we sit and stand, bow and process as if we really mean it? Do we listen attentively to the spoken and sung word and to the times of silence? Do we pray in one voice with others in the assembly?

What are your thoughts about the assembly's ministry of praying well? What would you add to the list about what it means and how it might enrich the Sunday celebration?

The work of creating and participating in symbols

We have already done some thinking about symbols in chapter 3. To recap, we said that symbols put us in touch with our deepest feelings and give us ways to express them. Symbols also have many meanings, so they can speak to many different people at different times in life. They might hold out new ways of thinking or acting, so they can actually change us. Religious symbols offer us ways to encounter the Mystery of God. And yes, we need to imagine! Symbols ask us to discover the meanings that lie beneath the surface of things.

We also said in chapter 3 that our Sunday worship wraps us in symbols—such as gestures, words, actions, objects, and people—but that we also need to *participate* in the symbols. This is a key part of our work as the assembly, and it also overlaps with what we have just said about praying well. How do we *participate* in symbols?

Recall our examples of common symbols in the last chapter: a wedding ring, a nation's flag, a memorial site, and a national anthem. If we are to find meaning in these symbols, we need to interact with them. A wedding ring grabs the heart of the person wearing it when he looks at or feels it and thinks of his wife. Her home country's flag brings tears to her eyes when she sees it flying on a pole outside the United Nations building. A Vietnam War veteran walks along the memorial wall on the National Mall in Washington, D.C., and places his fingers on the engraved names of his friends. Rather than watching the celebrity sing a solo, the crowd joins in the singing of the national anthem before the opening pitch at the baseball game. When we participate in symbols, we use our voices and our bodies, employ our senses, get our hearts involved, and tap our gift of imagination.

Recall experiences you have had of interacting with symbols, similar to those named above. What were the symbols and how did you participate in them? How did your participation affect you?

_____

_____

_____

_____

_____

_____

Symbols can be ever so familiar; we tend to claim them and have no need for step-by-step instructions to know how to interact with them. However, symbols can also grow and change because of our participation in them. We even create new symbols. Take, for example, a family meal. What happens when a family meal is a wedding rehearsal dinner? The meal ritual takes on new meaning and maybe new symbols when the family is expanded to include the spouse-to-be and his family. Or a friend's young daughters had three favorite bedtime stories, and the story of the evening had be one of these three. The stories were so familiar that the girls could finish the sentences, but there was always something new about the ritual. It was a new evening, winding down a day with new experiences. The time spent with their parents strengthened family relationships. As the girls grew, the bedtime story ritual became a ritual quiet time, bringing the day's happenings to prayer.

Of course, we choose whether we are going to participate in the symbols we encounter. At times we might resist or refuse to take part in them. For instance, maybe we go with friends to a rally in support of a certain cause, but we choose to stand away from the crowd and not take part in any of the activities. The rally still goes on, but perhaps we would have discovered that if we had participated, the experience would have been richer for us and for the others who gathered.

At other times a symbol simply might not speak to us. Not every symbol we encounter will. For example, there are many symbols of team spirit in sports, but if we're not fans, the pre-game rituals won't do much for us. Then again, there might be occasions when something does not seem to have meaning for us at that very moment, but when we encounter the same symbol at another time in life, it does carry meaning for us. We go to a college graduation ceremony of our parents' best friend's son and feel uninvolved. A couple of years later, a graduation ritual takes on new meaning when *we* are wearing the caps and gowns and walking in procession.

All this is what makes symbols so rich and amazing. When we are actively present to and participate in them, they can take hold of us and help us find meaning in life. If we resist them, they might not have much to say to us. Sometimes it's only later that we discover meaning in the symbols we encounter. And yes, symbols are very familiar; we learn them by interacting with them. Yet, they can suddenly seem unfamiliar and take us by surprise. They might change and offer new meanings, and new ones might even be created as people participate in them.

Have you ever had the experience of a symbolic object or activity carrying one meaning for you and a very different meaning for someone else? If so, describe what happened.

———————————————————————————————

———————————————————————————————

———————————————————————————————

———————————————————————————————

———————————————————————————————

———————————————————————————————

Let's now take what we know and have experienced regarding everyday symbols and look at the symbols we are invited to participate in during Sunday Mass, keeping in mind that our liturgical symbols are meant to lead us to encounter the Mystery of God.

First, our active presence is once again requested. The symbols of our eucharistic celebrations are there for our participation in them. Are we actively present to them, paying attention to what meaning they might have for us that day as individuals and as a faith community? Do we take part it them, allowing our bodies, minds, hearts, and imaginations to be fully involved? For instance, we enter the doors of the church, place our fingers in the baptismal font, and sign ourselves thoughtfully. We bow or genuflect before the altar. We use our voices to sing and pray with commitment. We listen to the word proclaimed as though we were sitting "on the edge of our seats." We say "Amen" with conviction as we receive the Body and Blood of Christ.

In what other ways can we actively participate in the many symbols of the Mass?

———————————————————————————————

———————————————————————————————

———————————————————————————————

———————————————————————————————

———————————————————————————————

———————————————————————————————

Next, we might wonder whether our liturgical symbols grow and change, as other kinds of symbols do. Can new ones be created? Absolutely. Like all symbols, the symbols of the church's liturgy are not frozen; they are full of life because human beings are involved and especially because Christ's Spirit is actively working in and through the symbols we experience. For example, the style of music for liturgical celebrations changes as a parish becomes more ethnically diverse. The preparation of the gifts has a different feel to it when food for the poor is carried in procession with the gifts of bread and wine. Our experience of the cross is different on Palm Sunday than it is on Easter Sunday. We bless ourselves with water from the baptismal font when we arrive for Sunday Mass, but this powerful symbol takes on new meanings when we celebrate a baptism.

You have already named ways in which you actively participate in the symbols of the Mass. Have there been times when these symbols have grown or changed?

_____

_____

_____

_____

_____

_____

As with other kinds of symbols, we have a choice when it comes to the symbols of the Mass. We can take part or keep our distance. If we put ourselves into the experience and are open to finding meaning in the symbols we meet, there's a good chance that we will find meaning, even if we don't realize it immediately. If we choose to keep our distance, the community will still pray and engage the symbols; however, our experience and that of the entire community would be enriched by our participation.

And finally, it is important to realize that not every symbol will speak to us at every Mass, and there might be some symbols of our worship that will never seem to attract us. Remember, the church's liturgy is packed with symbols, so there are many opportunities for us to participate and find meaning in the symbols we meet. It's best not to rule anything out; we never know when something might take us by surprise! All we as the assembly need to do is to come with open minds and hearts and be actively present to the celebration, for this is important work that we do.

And sometimes there is even more work to do . . .

Just when we might think that we could not possibly do more work as the Sunday assembly, we discover that we are asked to do just that! Additional responsibilities arise for the assembly when we celebrate particular rites of initiation, like infant baptism, the rituals of the Rite of Christian Initiation for Adults (RCIA), or First Communion. On occasion there might be anointing of the sick or a wedding during Sunday Mass. Various blessings are also common, such as the blessing of a couple on their golden wedding anniversary or of someone about to begin missionary work or go off to school, for example. The Sunday assembly is needed for all these rites. Our active presence is again needed.

What our work does for us

Like other work we do in life, our work as the Sunday assembly influences us in various ways. It helps us take on the attitudes of Christ—to be more and more Christlike in our way of being, thinking, and doing. Our work at Sunday Mass also brings us to realize more and more that the Spirit who dwells in our hearts directs our lives. We are constantly being prepared to be the Body of Christ in the world, to be disciples who preach the Good News and carry out the mission of the church. We turn now to exploring how Sunday Mass prepares us for our work in the world and how our work in the world prepares us to celebrate Eucharist.

CHAPTER 5

The Mass Is Ended—Now What?

We made the decision to go to Sunday Mass. We brought with us our stories, our life "stuff," our expectancy and active presence, our imaginations and concern for the world. Having celebrated Eucharist together, we have a little better understanding of ourselves as the assembly and of the work we do at Sunday Mass. So we've arrived at the end. Our work is done. Time to go. Right? Well, yes and no. True, we have a "concluding rite"; we hear "The Mass is ended"; we are dismissed. But is this an end or a beginning or something in-between? Is our work as a eucharistic assembly all said and done, or does it continue as we go about the rest of the week? It is time to "go," but what does "go" really mean here?

We can begin to take up these questions by taking a closer look at what we know as the concluding rite of the Mass. This part of the Mass is very brief, so brief that at times it might escape our attention, especially if we are searching the hymnal for the closing song or anxiously wanting to get on with our plans for the day. At the same time, it's ritual; we have rehearsed it often and know it well. It's a familiar symbol that packs a lot of meaning, and I suggest that the concluding rite can help us answer "The Mass is ended—now what?"

"The Lord be with you"

You might ask, "Haven't we exchanged this same greeting a few times already? Why now as we are ready to head out the door?" True, this exchange of greeting between the presider and the rest of the assembly happens during the gathering rite (after the sign of the cross the priest may say "The Lord be with you" or one of a couple longer options); the Liturgy of the Word (before the gospel is proclaimed); the Liturgy of the Eucharist (as we begin praying the Eucharistic Prayer); and now as we begin the concluding rite. I like to think of this dialogue as a sort of hinge that gets our attention and then draws us into what comes next in the celebration. But why do it at the end of Mass when we will soon be leaving the church?

Maybe this question is best answered with another question. What does this ancient ritual exchange of "The Lord be with you" say to us? In many ways it's as much an invitation as it is a greeting. Notice that the words are not "The Lord *is* with you" but "the Lord *be* with you." We are *asked* to believe, again and again, that as a praying assembly, Christ is present *in us* and working *through us*. Liturgy is always about invitation: God invites and we are asked to accept.

Throughout the celebration we have been asked to accept the invitation to be actively present to Christ's presence in the assembly. We talked about our identity as the Body of Christ and the church in chapter 3 ("Who *are* all these people?"). It's an *active* identity, somewhat like other shared identities we have, such as family, neighborhood, parish, workplace, and community, as well as our individual identities, such as spouse, parent, child, sibling, single person, religious, friend, or worker. Since these identities involve relationships and maybe even promises, something is required of us in order to live up to these names, including regularly recommitting ourselves to them. So, too, with our shared identity as the Body of Christ and the church. Relationships—with God, others, and all God has created—are key. Promises—our baptismal ones—are involved. As we have already discussed, something is required of us to live up to our name. And to help us remember this, we claim our name again and again. The greeting, "The Lord be with you," is one of our liturgical symbols (and memory aids) that invites us to do just that: to claim our name so that it is as much a part of us as our heartbeat.

Why this invitation, then, as the assembly gets set to leave the church and go our separate ways? Is it so that by the time we are told to "go," we are not tempted to think that our identity as the Body of Christ and the church can be taken off like a nametag? Is it to embolden us to live up to our name as we go about living our lives the rest of the week? Is it so that we are encouraged to be the face of Christ to a world in need of hope?

What do you hear when "The Lord be with you" is exchanged during the concluding rite of the Mass?

"May almighty God bless you . . ."

We likely know the words by heart: "May almighty God bless you, the Father, and the Son, and the Holy Spirit. Amen." And the gesture that these words accompany, the sign of the cross, is second nature to us Christians. We call it the "*final* blessing," but is it really *final*? Does it actually complete our work as assembly, or does our participation in this ritual blessing launch us into the daily work of Christian living? For a woman at a small inner city parish, the final blessing is a weekly point of departure; it has captured her imagination and made a difference in how she approaches everyday life:

> I guess you could say it's one of my regular daily prayers. A few years ago I caught myself repeating the final blessing to myself as I went about my day, so I made it my prayer. Actually, the words come to me first thing in the morning when I look in the mirror. I then say to myself, "I am blessed," and pray that I speak and act accordingly that day. The words often come to mind when I am with the people in my life. I whisper "May almighty God bless you . . ." and make the sign of the cross in the direction of my teenagers as they head off to school. I prayed this blessing the other day when my husband and I had to work through a disagreement. It has been with me this week as I deal with difficulties at work. The words of this blessing were the only words I could find to speak the other day when I hugged a friend after her chemotherapy treatment. I frequently pray this blessing when I help out at the neighborhood women's shelter. Often when I watch the evening news, the words reassure me that God is still at work, even in the midst of tragedies and suffering. But you know, these words also challenge me, whether they come at the end of Mass when I am standing with other parishioners or during moments of personal prayer. I wonder what it really

means to say "Amen" to this blessing and at the same time make the sign of the cross. An "Amen" always means we are agreeing to something, and to me the sign of the cross says, "Remember your baptism and Christian responsibilities." Maybe we're saying, "Yes, God, bless us, so that we are able to do what we can to better the world."

I think this woman's story helps answer the question about whether the final blessing at Mass marks the completion or the beginning of something. It's really "both/and," isn't it? In one sense, the final blessing feels like a "wrapping up" moment; at the same time, it "unwraps" the day-to-day living out of the Eucharist we just celebrated. In other words, we leave Mass and live as blessed people.

Allow the final blessing of the Mass to be your prayer as you go about your day. As these words come to you, what do you notice about how you respond to people and to what is happening? What does our "Amen" to the final blessing say to you? What does making the sign of the cross as part of this ritual say to you?

———————————————————————————

———————————————————————————

———————————————————————————

———————————————————————————

———————————————————————————

"Go in peace . . ."

Finally, we are dismissed. The presiding priest or assisting deacon announces: "Go in the peace of Christ," "The Mass is ended, go in peace," or "Go in peace to love and serve the Lord." (Occasionally, these options get combined, such as "The Mass is ended, go in peace to love and serve the Lord.") The other members of the assembly respond: "Thanks be to God." Again, the questions: Is this an end or a beginning or something in-between? Is our work as a eucharistic assembly finished *now*? We are dismissed, but what about the commands we hear? How has our participation in the eucharistic celebration prepared us to "go," "love," and "serve"? And what are we really saying when we respond to these commands with "Thanks be to God"?

"The Mass is ended . . ."

True, this particular Sunday liturgy has ended; yet, rather than a conclusion, I think of this announcement as another turning point. "The Mass is ended" are words that turn us outward, preparing us to hear and act on the commands of "go," "love," and "serve." As a hinge, the announcement, "The Mass is ended," indicates that our leaving Mass and what follows as we carry on with daily living are not separate actions. In other words, Sunday Mass is not a stand-alone occasion; rather, it is woven into the very fabric of Catholic life.

This idea also highlights Eucharist as an ongoing sacrament, meaning that the sacrament does not begin and end in an hour-long Mass. As people who have celebrated together, who have responded to the word proclaimed and feasted at the table of the Lord, the sacrament continues *in us.* The assembly as sacrament is, as we have said before, "a visible sign of the gift of God's Self to the world." Enabled by the Spirit, we continuously grow in this identity. Like other significant roles we have—disciple, worker, spouse, parent, friend, global citizen, for instance—our becoming a visible sign of God's saving activity is a process. Participation in the Eucharist is vital to this process; it keeps us growing!

"Go . . ."

Notice that it's not "Good-bye" or "Have a nice day" or "Thanks for coming. See you next week." It's "Go." We are sent, dispatched, pushed out. Just as God called us together, God now sends us forth. We are eucharistic people with work to do, so we are told to "go," do it. What exactly is this work of ours, and are we ready for it? In a nutshell, it's the work of discipleship. It's the work we signed up for when we were baptized and the work we recommit ourselves to when we celebrate the Eucharist. I know that this might be a little intimidating. We might not even be all that comfortable with the word "discipleship." I think of the New Testament stories about Jesus' disciples and wonder, "Do I have enough faith and courage to be like them?" Yet, as the baptized, that is what we are—disciples of Jesus Christ. As followers of Christ, we learn from him, accept his teachings, and assist with the work of telling the world the Good News of God's generous love in Jesus Christ and the Spirit.

What would you say is the work of Christian discipleship? How do you personally and as a faith community assist with the work of sharing the Good News?

_____

_____

_____

_____

_____

_____

How do we get ready to do this work? What prepares us? I think we have available to us several sources, including prayer, reading the Scriptures, conversations with our spiritual companions, reaching out to those in need, spiritual reading, involvement with issues of social concern, and, of course, liturgy. Sunday Eucharist prepares us in many ways to do the work of Christian discipleship. The preparation is usually subtle; we might not even be conscious of it. Yet, our regular participation in the Eucharist helps ready us to "go" and do our work. How and when does this happen? Consider these ideas:

- "It's often the Scripture readings for me. I grow in my understanding of Christ's teachings and mission by listening to the word, and I think about what is required of me to live the gospel."

- "Praying with other people reminds me that I can't just live for me. I think it was St. Paul who wrote that Christians live not for themselves but for others. Being part of the Sunday assembly makes me conscious of this. It shakes me out of my self-concern and attunes me to the fact that I am connected to a global community. This brings tough questions: How do I act toward others? What are my attitudes and values? Do I value other people and show concern for them? Do I help others without expecting that I'll get something out of it for myself?"

- "Participating in Communion is what nourishes me most. Sharing in the one Bread and the one Cup feeds and strengthens me. When the Communion minister says, 'The Body of Christ' and 'The Blood of Christ,' and I eat and drink, I feel empowered. It gives me courage to live as a Christian."

- "I marvel at our reverence for the things of the earth that we use at Mass: water, bread, wine, fire, and sometimes oil. It impresses upon me how important it is for us to be good stewards of creation."

- "As a priest, I have the privilege of preaching on the word. I try at times to work principles of Catholic social teaching into my homilies.

Reflecting on these principles and relating them to our call to discipleship certainly helps me see and respond to the needs of the community, local and global."

*What would you add to the list? When and how does the Eucharist prepare you
to do the work of Christian discipleship?*

_____

_____

_____

_____

_____

"Go in the peace of Christ . . . to love and serve . . ."

As I write this, it is August of 2006. Relationships in the world are com-
plex; daily events are often alarming and heartbreaking. The Middle East is
in crisis. War and other violence continue to plague the people of Iraq and
Afghanistan. Peace negotiations in Darfur and Northern Uganda are shaky
at best; meanwhile, the senseless killings and kidnappings go on. And these
are not the only places where there is strife. It seems many people live in
fear—of terrorism, disease, abuse, weather-related disasters, lack of employ-
ment, to name only a few. Far too many people live in poverty and lack the
basics: shelter, food, clothing, heath care, an education, and work. Many
families are stressed and struggle to maintain healthy relationships. These
are also unsettled times in the Catholic Church: the clergy abuse scandal
has shaken trust; differences of opinion about church teachings or ways of
doing things sometimes lead to unkind finger-pointing; many parishes have
been closed or merged, often causing great distress for parishioners.

And yet, every Sunday we hear "Go *in peace.*" What does this mean to
us when all around us peace appears to be lacking? Maybe we even struggle
to find peace within ourselves, in our family, parish, neighborhood, or
workplace. Still, we are told, "Go in the peace of Christ."

*We know from our own experiences what peace is. We have a deep sense of
when it exists and when it is lacking. Think for a moment about your experi-*

ences of peace. What was or is right about those experiences? When peace was or is absent, what was or is missing?

_____

_____

_____

_____

_____

_____

I have a hunch that a common theme surfaced as you talked about your experiences, that is, relationships were involved. For example, you might have talked about your relationship with God. Maybe you spoke about your relationships with your family members, neighbors, or co-workers. Your relationship with yourself might have also been one of the experiences you named. You might also have spoken about relationships between nations and peoples within nations. Peace does seem to be rooted in right relationships, doesn't it? Another word we can use to speak about right relationships is "justice." Justice and peace go hand in hand.

Right relationships are what we celebrate at Mass. Our participation in Eucharist immerses us in justice, in what it means to live in right relationship with God, ourselves, other people, and all of creation. This is the peace of Christ. At Mass we are formed in justice and peace, and we are prepared to work for justice and peace in our personal relationships and in the wider world. When does this formation and preparation happen? Gradually, for again, it's a process. How does it happen? In the same ways we are prepared for the work of Christian discipleship, since justice and peace lie at the heart of this work. So, we can look back a few pages at our list of the ways Eucharist prepares us for our work as disciples. Allow me to suggest a few ideas:

- *Praying with the assembly.* Yes, that "mixed bunch" we gather with every Sunday. Different in so many ways, and yet we have so much in common, from basic human needs to our baptism in Christ, the need for forgiveness to God's call to holiness of life. Although diverse, we are one Body of Christ. This one Body, standing before God, praying in and through Jesus Christ and the Holy Spirit, is where we get a glimpse of what right relationships look like. How, then, might this glimpse of right relationships impact our relationship with God, others, and all of creation? What attitudes and values do we absorb?

• *Hospitality.* Remember this from the last chapter? We talked about hospitality as making room for others, welcoming the stranger, and receiving someone as we would Christ. Hospitality concerns relationships, so our experience of hospitality at Sunday Mass can prepare us to be ministers of justice and peace.

• *The Word.* The Scriptures are a main source of learning about the justice and peace God desires. Let us actively listen, while sitting "on the edge of our seats." What do we hear from Sunday to Sunday?

• *The prayers.* The words we pray at Mass help us to imagine what justice and peace mean. For example, pay close attention to the Eucharistic Prayer, the general intercessions, the opening prayer and prayer after communion, the Lord's Prayer. What can be learned from these texts?

• *The sign of peace.* This ritual gesture that we rehearse each week has a lot to say about the peace of Christ. We first pray that we be granted the peace and unity that is the kingdom of God. And then we extend this same peace to one another; we speak it, we might offer our hand or an embrace. Again the question: What does this tell us about right relationships?

What's on your list of the ways our eucharistic celebrations prepare us to be ministers of justice and peace?

_____

_____

_____

_____

_____

_____

We began this section by pointing to where peace is lacking in our world and our church. I think it's important to return to this, for the absence of peace, while it coexists with the presence of peace, is a harsh reality that we face. The challenges for us to love and serve the Lord as ministers of justice and peace can be immense. We might wonder whether it's even possible to imagine possibilities for justice and peace in light of so much turmoil in the world. How do we handle this and remain steadfast in our belief that with the Holy Spirit working in and through us, we can be a sign of Christ's justice and peace in our times? Once again, I can only offer a few thoughts for your consideration, all of which are rooted in the Eucharist.

What first comes to mind is the *paschal mystery.* Every Sunday we remember the life, death, and resurrection of Jesus Christ. The paschal mystery is present to us, reminding us that Jesus Christ defeated death so that we may have life. For Christians, the paschal mystery deeply shapes our take on life; it influences how we look upon times of darkness and dying in our own lives and in the world. It is what helps us peer through the darkness and see the light of Christ. This is the basis of our hope and the source of our courage to be instruments of Christ's justice and peace.

As I have said before, a sacramental imagination is key. Our participation in Mass exercises this imagination, even stretches it so it can grow. A sacramental imagination enables us to see God revealed in the ordinariness of life and to recognize where right relationships have taken hold, where justice and peace are the norm. The experiences of peace you named earlier confirm that right relationships can and do happen. How important it is, then, for us to draw attention to these signs of hope. A sacramental imagination also allows us to imagine and realize what's possible, for God is always present, even when it seems that justice and peace are absent. With God, change is always possible; justice and peace are possible.

The Sunday assembly further impresses upon us that we don't go it alone. The work of discipleship, the work of justice and peace, is shared work. Yes, we are also individuals with unique ways to love and serve the Lord, but as baptized people, we are equally a community. We can draw inspiration and support from one another. We help one another to pray well; we can also help one another to live well.

Finally, as Christians we believe that this world is not all there is; there is more to come. The reign of God is already but not yet. In other words, the fulfillment of God's reign is yet to come. Our eucharistic celebrations help us to remember this.

What are your thoughts about the ways in which the Eucharist can help us remain hopeful, point to the evidence of justice and peace, and continue to work for justice and peace where they are lacking?

"Thanks be to God"

We have been given our commands: "Go in peace," "love," and "serve." "Thanks be to God!" What are we saying here? Are we saying, "Thanks be to God that we have work to do, a mission in the world, that our ministry as assembly, our identity as the Body of the Christ and the church must continue as we live our lives?" Once we give thanks, the assembly moves out in procession to love and serve the Lord.

Our Sunday celebration begins another week. Having just assembled to share the Eucharist, how will our lives and our world be better off this week? How will our life experiences and the opportunities to love and serve prepare us, even change us, for our work as we assemble again next Sunday? Our preparation for Sunday Mass week after week is to live our lives by living up to our name. And when next Sunday arrives, we will have another decision to make: to go or not to go to Mass. We will have "stuff" to bring, which, because we have done another week's worth of living, will be different than that of the previous Sunday.

We will gather with the church, the Body of Christ, and we will know that we're there because we haven't finished all that we need to do. We will know the need to be nourished for the work of discipleship at the table of the Lord, with both word and sacrament. So we say, "Thanks be to God" for calling us back into assembly, to celebrate the work we have done and the work we have before us as we live as people baptized in Christ. May the Lord be with us.